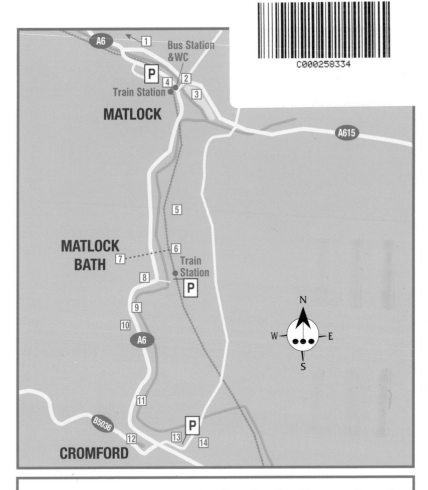

Matlock, Matlock Bath & Cromford

1. Arc Leisure Centre
2. Crown Square
3. Hall Leys Park
4. Peak Rail
5. High Tor
6. Cable Car
7. Heights of Abraham

8. Aquarium
9. Peak District Mining Museum
10. Gulliver's Kingdom
11. Masson Mill
12. Cromford Mill Pond
13. Old Mill
14. Cromford Wharf

Front cover: Matlock Bath **Back cover top (l-r):** Hall Ley's Park, Matlock; Steam train at Matlock station
Back cover main: Masson Mill

A view of Matlock from the High Tor footpath

MATLOCK, MATLOCK BATH & CROMFORD

Matlock

It is appropriate that Derbyshire County Council should have its headquarters in the town of Matlock. The name of the place comes from the Old English *Meslach* and probably means 'the oak where the moot was held.' It would therefore seem that local government has been administrated from this place on the River Derwent ('the river of oaks') for over 900 years.

John Smedley's huge **Hydro,** where the County Council now meets, still lords it over the town from the Matlock Bank hillside where it was built in 1853. It is an amazing building – from the front (south) with its terraced gardens (now mainly a car park for council employees) and central domed tower topped with an ironwork corona, it looks like nothing less than an enormous seaside hotel, stranded far inland. But from the rear the building, linked by a covered bridge across Smedley Street, takes on the appearance of a grim industrial factory.

Smedley (see box p.4/5) was the man who founded modern Matlock, promoting it in the 19th century as a centre for the then-fashionable cure of hydrotherapy. This involved all kinds of showers and other bathing contraptions, and the appliance of copious amounts of spring water at various temperatures.

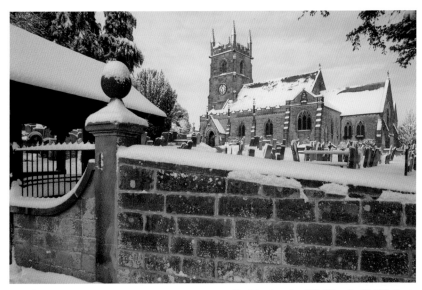

Parish church of St Giles in Old Matlock

John Smedley (1803-1874)

John Smedley, Matlock's pioneer of hydrotherapy, was born in Wirksworth. He originally worked in his grandfather's textile mill at Lea Mills, which still makes exclusive knitwear. But John suffered bouts of depression and while on honeymoon on a tour of Europe, he contracted typhus and malaria.

He was cured after a visit to the hydrotherapy establishment at Ben Rhydding, Ilkley, in 1849, and he came back enthused by what he had seen and experienced. His four-storey Matlock Hydro, which has served since 1955 as Derbyshire County Council's offices, was begun in 1853 and continuously extended until 1901.

His hydropathic 'patients' included some of the great names of Victorian England, such as Robert Louis Stevenson, Ivor Novello, Sir

Thomas Beecham and comedians Harry Lauder and George Robey.

Smedley also designed Riber Castle, the fairy tale, castellated folly which overlooks Matlock, intending to live in it. It was to be topped by an observatory tower 225ft/68m high, but it was never finished. After many years standing half-finished and empty, it is now being converted into residential accommodation. Smedley died in 1874.

Smedley's Hydro, now the headquarters of Derbyshire County Council

Patients reached Smedley's Hydro up the very steep Bank Road and Rutland Street by cabled-hauled tramcars, said to be the steepest tramway on a public road in the world. The Matlock trams became quite a famous tourist attraction and ran safely for 34 years until the lines were taken up in 1927. The pretty little Tramway Shelter, surmounted by a clock, still stands in the Hall Leys Park riverside public gardens.

Smedley's initiative attracted others, and at the turn of the century, there were over 20 hydropathic establishments in the town. Another, Wyvern House Hydro, later became the Ernest Bailey Comprehensive School.

Close to the Hydro is **All Saints Church**, built in 1883, which has a beautiful east window dating from 1905, designed by Edward Burne-Jones and made by the William Morris Company.

No less than eight hamlets make up the modern town of Matlock, including the original settlement of Old Matlock on the hillside to the east of the river, where a charming 18th century rectory can be found next to the former Wheatsheaf Farm, which dates from 1681.

The **parish church of St Giles** in Old Matlock has a 15th century Perpendicular tower, but most of the rest was rebuilt in the 19th century, although the font is Norman. Six paper 'maidens' or garlands, hang in the church as at Ashford-in-the-Water, commemorating girls who died before marriage.

Matlock Bridge over the powerful River Derwent dates from the 15th century, but has been widened to take modern traffic. The main A6 and its traffic, was mercifully diverted away from the town centre and bridge in 2007 when the Matlock bypass was opened. Crown Square, topped by its somewhat incongruous modern stainless steel 'crown' in the middle of the roundabout by the bridge, is the centrepiece of the modern town. Another main shopping area is in Dale Road, which leads down the A6 towards Matlock Bath.

Steam buffs love the experience of travelling in a steam train on **Peak Rail's** restored section of the former Midland Line between Matlock and Rowsley. When the line closed in 1968, a group of enthusiasts restored it to its former glory, and there are ambitious plans to restore the whole line and take it through the heart of the Peak District National Park. Peak Rail stages various special events throughout the year, and especially popular are the Santa and Steam Specials at Christmas. Trains – both steam and diesel-hauled – run at weekends and certain weekdays all year, ☎ 01629 580381 for details.

Lord Seb Coe, the chairman of London's 2012 Olympic bid, opened

Top: Hall Leys Park in summer

Above left: Steam train at Matlock station

Above: Lord Seb Coe opening the Arc Lesiure Centre

Left: Penny fartthing racing in Hall Leys Park

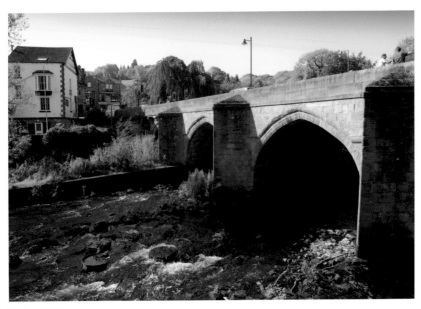

Matlock Bridge

Matlock's latest attraction, the futuristic £12 million **Arc Leisure Centre** in Bakewell Road, Matlock, in October, 2011. The up-to-the-minute facilities include a 25-metre, eight-lane swimming pool plus a teaching pool and toddler splash pad; badminton courts; a sports hall and a state-of-the-art, 50-station fitness suite. There are also spaces for fitness classes, indoor hockey, basketball, volleyball, five-a-side football, netball, gymnastics and dance classes, plus a café and meeting rooms.

Matlock Bath

Matlock Bath on a summer Sunday has been called the Blackpool of the Peak District. It has become a popular destination for motor-cyclists, and the bikers can often be seen sunning themselves and admiring each other's machines along the South Parade by the river.

The town has been a tourist trap since the health-giving properties of its warm springs were discovered in the late 17th century. The original attraction may have been the lime and salt-rich solutions from the springs which coat anything they come into contact with in a spongy rock known as tufa. The Wishing or Petrifying Well near the Pavilion and Temple Road car park is a good example.

Matlock Bath occupies the bottom of the steep-sided **Derwent Gorge**, with the great 300ft (90m) limestone shield of **High Tor** overshadowing everything. This is a popular resort for serious rock-climbers, who can often be seen hanging apparently effortlessly from its smooth, blank wall of rock like spiders on a wall.

On the other side of the river, the wooded slopes of the **Heights of Abraham** (named after General James Wolfe's famous battle at Quebec in 1759) can be reached much more easily but just as spectacularly by the **Cable Cars.** These swing up from Joseph Paxton's Swiss chalet-style former Matlock Bath Station (now the Whistlestop Centre of the Derbyshire Wildlife Trust), to the castellated Victoria Prospect Tower which marks the summit.

Once you get up to the Heights there are plenty of things to do. A guided tour through the **Great Masson Cavern** will take you from the flickering light of a lead miner's candle to the awe-inspiring sight of

Above: Matlock Bath Illuminations
Below: Cable cars, Matlock Bath

Left: Peak District Mining Museum **Right:** Inside Temple Mine

the whole cavern awash with colour. The **Great Rutland Cavern** was formerly the Nestus lead mine. Here you can experience the lives of the 17th century lead miners who first discovered these caves.

Other attractions on the Heights include the **Fossil Factory,** home to the fossilised remains of a giant, three-metre long ichthyosaur, from the days when dinosaurs ruled the earth. Both fossils and geology are brought to life in this fascinating new visitor experience.

Both the Great Rutland and Masson Caverns are former lead mines. They have been opened up for visitors to enjoy the underground splendours of the many caves which riddle the Heights of Abraham.

Back down in the town, the **Royal Cave and Temple Mine** are former flourspar workings which are also open to visitors, near the fascinating **Peak District Mining Museum** (☎ 01629 583834; www.peakmines. co.uk). This is housed in the pink-painted **Pavilion**, originally built in 1885 when Matlock Bath was at its height as a popular spa town.

The fascinating story of lead mining in the Peak is told through various interactive exhibits in the museum, including a replica lead mine shaft which children can descend to get a feel of what it actually felt like to be a lead miner. The major exhibit in the museum, which is also the headquarters of the Peak District Mines Historical Society, is the large water-pressure engine rescued from a local lead mine and dated 1819.

Children love the rides in the magical themed areas of **Gulliver's Theme Park**, set on a hillside overlooking Matlock Bath (☎ 01925 444888; www.gulliversfun.co.uk) just off the A6 in Temple Walk.

The **New Bath Hotel** on the A6, where John Ruskin stayed in 1829, also dates from the period of Matlock Bath's prominence as a spa, as does the elegant spire of the **parish church of the Holy Trinity**, which was built in 1842.

But the most beautiful piece of ecclesiastical architecture in Matlock Bath is the little hillside **Chapel of St John the Baptist** on Cliff Road high above the village. This was built in 1897 to a design by Sir Guy Dawber as a chapel-of-ease, and its medieval-looking turrets and oriel windows are matched inside by a rood screen, reredos, and exuberantly-painted walls.

The coming of the railway to Matlock Bath in 1849 gave a great boost to its emerging tourist industry, and the line still connects to the main line at Derby, 14miles/22km away, and thence to London.

Cromford

Cromford, two miles south of Matlock, marks the northern gateway to the Derwent Valley Mills World Heritage Site. Its story is inextricably linked with that of Richard Arkwright, the semi-literate genius who transformed England from an agricultural nation into the leader of the Industrial Revolution in the latter years of the 18th century (see box p.12). If it had been a little easier of access and not situated deep in the Derbyshire hills, Cromford could even have rivalled Manchester as the cradle of the Industrial Revolution.

Mill Pond, Cromford village

Sir Richard Arkwright (1732-1792)

Generally acknowledged to be one of the founders of the Industrial Revolution and the inventor of the modern industrial factory system, Sir Richard Arkwright was born in Preston in 1792. He began his career as an apprentice barber and later became a dyer of hair for wig making.

Top: Old Mill, Cromford **Above:** Wharf, Cromford Canal

When the fashion for wigs fell out of favour, he turned his attention to textiles and developed a cotton spinning frame (later renamed the water frame after the switch to water power) in the late 1760s. He built the world's first water-powered cotton mill at Cromford in 1771. The mill complex and another of his mills, Masson Mill, now form part of the UNESCO-designated Derwent Valley World Heritage Site.

Unlike many 18th century employers, Arkwright looked after his workers, building terraced cottages for them near his mills at Cromford, and he also built the imposing Greyhound public house. Arkwright originally lived at Rock House in Cromford. He then started to build the imposing Grade II Willersley Castle, on the banks of the Derwent. A fire broke out during its construction, and Arkwright died in 1792 before work on the building was complete. He is buried in St Mary's parish church.

Arkwright came to Cromford in 1771 to utilise the power of the River Derwent and build the world's first water-powered cotton mill at what is now known as the **Old Mill**, just off the A6 in Mill Lane. Now open to the public as a visitor centre, this fortress-like building was designed to deter would-be Luddites who wished to destroy the new machinery which they thought would take work from what had traditionally been a cottage industry. The mill is the site of the first water-powered cotton mill in the country, and the centrepiece of the Derwent Mills World Heritage Site (see box below), designated in 2001. Guided tours take you round the fascinating site, which is still in the course of restoration.

The Derwent Valley Mills World Heritage Site

The Derwent Valley Mills obtained international recognition as a World Heritage Site in December 2001 at a meeting of UNESCO's World Heritage Committee in Helsinki. It was described as being of "outstanding universal value" because of the role the water-powered textile mills in the valley had played in the Industrial Revolution.

The site inscribed on the World Heritage List is made up of a 15 mile/24km length of the valley, stretching from Arkwright's Masson Mills in Matlock Bath to the Silk Mill in Derby's city centre. It encompasses the mills and their accompanying historic communities at Cromford, Lea, Belper and Milford.

The site is managed by a partnership made up of over 30 stakeholders. Derbyshire County Council has been the lead body within the Derwent Valley Mills Partnership since its inception in 2000. Much groundwork has been undertaken since then, with the production of a Management Plan, a Transportation Plan, an Economic Development Plan and a Tourism and Interpretation Plan.

Masson Mill

The bright red-brick and Venetian-windowed **Masson Mill**, on the A6, was built in 1784, and now houses the Masson Mill Megastore Shopping Outlet. You can still see the mill machinery in situ in the basement museum, and be whisked back two centuries to the days when cotton was king.

Arkwright's mock-Gothic **Willersley Castle**, just over Cromford's famous 15th century bridge across the Derwent, was built in 1782-88, and is now a Methodist residential centre. The ancient bridge is complete with a rare bridge chapel and an 18th century fishing pavilion.

Below Willersley Castle stands Cromford's **parish church of St Mary**, built on the orders of Arkwright in 1797. It is mainly in the Perpendicular style and contains the tomb of Richard Arkwright, the man who put Cromford so firmly on the map.

Willersley Castle

Across the limestone cutting known as Scarthin Nick there is a village school in the main part of the village to the west of the A6. In Greyhound Square, Arkwright provided the grand facade of the Greyhound Inn as somewhere for his workers' recreation after work. Behind Greyhound Square is Cromford's millpond, known as The Dam, a tranquil spot away from the rushing traffic, and the tiny and idiosyncratic Scarthin book shop overlooks the scene.

The best examples of Arkwright's high-quality accommodation for his workers are to be found in the fine, three-storey stone-built terraces which contour up the hill in North Street.

Another famous name connected with Cromford is the popular childrens' book author, **Alison Uttley** (1884-1976), who was born at Castle Top Farm (private), where she lived until her late teens. Village life in Cromford in the late 19th century is meticulously recalled in her books *The Farm on the Hill*, and *The Country Child*, although Uttley is perhaps best known for her 'Little Grey Rabbit' and 'Sam Pig' stories.

The Crimean War heroine, **Florence Nightingale** – popularly known as the 'Lady of the Lamp' – lived for many years at Lea Hurst, Holloway, although she was born in Florence in 1820. She devoted her life to nursing and is best remembered as a pioneer in the profession and for devising effective sanitation methods for hospitals. Her most famous contribution came during the Crimean War, when she and 38 volunteer nurses were sent to Selimiye Barracks in Scutari, Turkey, to care for wounded British soldiers. Awarded the Royal Red Cross by Queen Victoria in 1883, in 1907 she became the first woman to receive the Order of Merit. Nightingale died peacefully in her sleep at Lea Green in 1910 the age of 90.

Running parallel to the River Derwent is the restored **Cromford Canal**, which linked with the ambitious Cromford and High Peak Railway (now the High Peak Trail). It was completed in 1831 to cross the high White Peak plateau to Whaley Bridge, at the beginning of the Railway Age. The canal and former railway are now enjoyed by leisure users. The canal is a Derbyshire Wildlife Trust nature reserve, famous for its water voles, and the railway is now the popular High Peak Trail walking and riding route.

Top: Cromford Canal

Above: A water vole, Cromford Canal

Cromford and High Peak Railway

The Cromford and High Peak railway line, which opened in 1830, aimed to link the Cromford Canal with the Peak Forest Canal at Whaley Bridge. It was originally designed as a canal, and the stations were called wharfs.

But this involved crossing the formidable 1,000ft/305m high White Peak limestone plateau. The engineer James Outram soon realised the gradients were too severe and the line started as the horse-drawn Peak Forest Tramway.

Motive power on the level sections was originally provided by horses, and on the steeper inclines, steam engines, such as that at the Middleton Top Engine House, hauled the wagons up by an ingenious continuous-cable balancing system.

The Cromford and High Peak Railway, which finally closed in 1967, boasted the steepest gradient (1:8½ at Middleton) and tightest curve (the 55-yard radius Gotham Curve), on any British railway.

FURTHER INFORMATION

Arc Leisure Matlock
Bakewell Road, Matlock
☎ 01629 581322; email:
arcleisurematlock@derbyshiredales.gov.uk

Gulliver's Theme Parks
Temple Walk, Matlock Bath
☎ 01925 444888; www.gulliversfun.co.uk

Heights of Abraham and Cable Cars
Matlock Bath
☎ 01629 582365;
www.heightsofabraham.com

Matlock Bath Aquarium
110 North Parade, Matlock Bath
☎ 01629 583624

Peak District Mining Museum
The Pavilion, South Parade, Matlock Bath
☎ 01629 583834; www.peakmines.co.uk

Peak Rail
Matlock Station, Matlock
☎ 01629 580381; www.peakrail.co.uk

Sir Richard Arkwright's Cromford Mills
Cromford Mill, Mill Lane, Cromford,
☎ 01629 823256;
www.arkwrightsociety.org.uk

Sir Richard Arkwright's Masson Working Textile Mills Museum
Derby Road, Matlock Bath
☎ 01629 581001; www.massonmills.co.uk

Events in the Matlock area

Matlock Farmers' Market: Imperial Rooms, Matlock, third Saturday of each month

Matlock Live! During June at various locations around the town

Matlock Bath Illuminations: During September and October

Christmas Market: Scarthin Promenade, Cromford, early December

Boxing Day Raft Race: On Boxing Day (December 26) annually, on the River Derwent between Cawdor Quarry and Cromford Meadows. There is a possibility this may be discontinued

Other useful information

Car Parks

Matlock: Bank Road; Matlock Station and Dale Road

Matlock Bath: Railway Station; Temple Walk and Pavilion

Cromford: Greyhound Square; Masson Mill; Cromford Mill; a free car park at Cromford Meadows

Public Toilets

Matlock: Bus station, Bakewell Road; and two in Hall Leys Park

Matlock Bath: North Parade adjacent to Midland Hotel and A6 car park; and entrance to Derwent Gardens

Cromford: The Memorial Garden; Cromford Wharf car park; High Peak Junction and Cromford Mill

Market Days

Matlock: Tuesdays and Fridays

All information is correct at the time of printing

Acknowledgements

Photography

© **Mark Titterton** Front cover; back cover left & bottom; p.2; p.3; p.4–5; p.7top & right; p.11; p.12all; p.13; p.15top © **Edward Rokita** p.5inset; p.9both © **Sheila Rayson** Back cover top-right; p.7middle-left © **Derbyshire Dales District Council** (derbyshiredales.gov.uk) p.7bottom © **Paul Deakin** p.10both © **Christian Guild** p.14top © **Shirley Freeman** p.15bottom © **Linda Bussey** p.8

Special thanks to
Visit Peak District, Peak District Tourist Information – www.visitpeakdistrict.com
Derbyshire Wildlife Trust – www.derbyshirewildlifetrust.org.uk
Peak Rail – www.peakrail.co.uk
Peak District Mining Museum – www.peakmines.co.uk

Published by **Ashbourne Editions**
10 Queen Elizabeth Court, Belle Vue Road, Ashbourne DE6 1NE
Tel: (01335) 344882 Mobile: 07890 854634

1st edition: ISBN: 978-1-873-775-43-1

© **Roly Smith 2012**

Print Gomer Press, Llandysul, Wales **Design** www.ceibagraphics.co.uk